HOW TO LOVE YOURSELF:

8 tips to believing in yourself and giving yourself the love you deserve

By Charles J. Smith

Table of contents

Introduction

Advice about loving oneself is all the rage these days. If you walk into your favorite neighborhood gift store, you'll probably discover Brene Brown self-compassion quotes embossed on pillows, self-love manifesting candles topped with rose quartz, and decks of positive affirmation cards. This advice frequently ignores the numerous complex reasons why someone might struggle with self-worth.

Self-love is a commodity. But are we buying it? Kat from Euphoria certainly isn't, but even if it seems corny or oversimplified, the majority of mental health specialists will tell you, in one way or another, that both your mental health and fulfilling relationships must be nicer and more accepting of yourself. However, several things (including trauma, years of self-criticism, and systemic prejudice, to mention a few) can make this seemingly straightforward technique far more difficult to implement.

Read on for helpful advice on how to (really) love oneself without the need for motivational sayings (but no shame if those help you, either).

CHAPTER 1

Trust yourself to make good decisions for yourself

The issue with the world is that smart individuals are full of uncertainties, while others with little intelligence are overconfident.

It's likely that you are smarter than your more outwardly confident coworkers if you often question yourself. You may take it as a compliment if you're one of the more insecure people among us.

It's unfortunate that intellect alone doesn't always lead to success in life. How many times have you seen someone who is inept but confident being promoted over someone who is quieter and more skilled? Take the workplace as an example.

Even while it doesn't always seem fair, the good news is that you can develop your self-confidence, which may subsequently have a favorable impact on how other people see you. Building inner strength via both serious self-reflection and basic everyday practices may help one become more self-assured and behave more like a leader.

Self-belief is important outside of the job as well. We all have an internal gatekeeper that we must go through while making choices. When you believe in yourself, you can make decisions without second-guessing. If you don't, making your commitment will be more difficult, and even if you do, you'll be second-guessing yourself for a while: "Did I really do the right thing?"

Making a significant choice without at least a little amount of self-doubt is quite uncommon. You can be worried about making the incorrect decision in a culture that doesn't readily accept errors. But have you ever thought about how poor self-esteem and worry about making decisions can be detrimental to your relationships, personal growth, and general wellbeing?

You can get through difficulties, accomplish your objectives, and improve at what you do by learning to trust yourself. Many leaders are sharp individuals who follow their instincts and stay true to their principles even in the face of opposition, having a significant impact as a consequence. There is no doubt that these qualities may be learned. You can do it too if they can.

In order to trust yourself, you must have faith in your own identity and judgments, which you might develop through time. Here are some of the most effective techniques for you to start developing self-confidence in your professional, personal, and other endeavors.

There are nine ways to increase your self-confidence: Move forth and believe in yourself.

1) Try to be as genuine as you can

You probably worry too much about what other people think if you question yourself all the time. You may have learned to present a perfect image of yourself to others, but in your heart of hearts, you are hesitant to exhibit who you really are. If you don't feel confident in who you are, people may see you as untrustworthy and inauthentic. After all, how can they trust you if you don't trust yourself?

It is simpler to fully trust someone the more we get to know them. The connection you have with yourself is no different. You must first understand who you are if you wish to trust yourself. What motivates you? What are you particularly skilled at? Being as honest with yourself as you can help you show your true self.

You shouldn't cling to what you believe is required of you. Each choice you make will feel more genuine than the previous if you let go of the traits and features that other people have forced onto you.

Keep your doubts from impeding your development. Doubt your doubts if you must, but only if you must. Say what you want to say, speak out, and let others know that your voice counts. You'll benefit from it more.

2) Pay attention to the inner voice
Paying careful attention to your inner voice is one method of really understanding how you feel about yourself. It's time to pause and pay close attention if your inner conversation mostly comprises of self-criticism and typically arouses unpleasant feelings.

Take a moment to consider where your self-deprecating thoughts are truly coming from the next time you catch yourself doing it. Then consider:

The voice's characteristics: Who is making decisions in your head? Do you hear your own voice, or is it your spouse, father, or employer speaking? This procedure will assist you in realizing that this voice isn't totally your own and doesn't need to be absorbed, despite the fact that it may seem stupid.

When the voice is most audible: Do you often second-guess yourself and your statements? Do you often reflect on discussions in which you might have spoken more but compromised yourself?

Keep in touch with this voice and write down any ideas that come to mind. Determine the identity of the voice's originator and note the precise minute at which it first emerged. Find a good character attribute for each bad one and place it next to it. Positive psychology emphasizes the need of reframing negative comments as objective observations since doing so may significantly enhance your wellbeing.

3) Be kind to yourself
Once you've recognized your inner voice, you must learn when to disregard it.

Your inner critic's judgments are not an accurate reflection of your value as a person.

Nobody is flawless. You'll never feel like you're enough if you allow your perfectionist side to take control; you'll always find fault with your actions, choices, and assessments.

The key to developing self-trust is practicing self-love and taking responsibility for both your successes and failures. The unwavering love a mother feels for her kid or the unwavering affection between brothers?

They are not dissimilar from the unwavering self-love required for self-confidence.

Don't allow self-criticism to control your emotions; instead, pay attention to your inner voice. Keep in mind that you deserve love and that you are where it all starts. Building self-confidence and self-trust will be simpler the more kind to yourself.

4) Quit second-guessing your actions.
As a defining characteristic when assessing your internal frame of reference, assertiveness is a quality that many leaders possess. Even—and especially—when such judgments seem to be ill-advised or contentious, great leaders make them and adhere to their principles. The advantages of following your intuition and gut instincts are well supported by research.

Though self-criticism isn't necessarily a negative thing, it may be a symptom of insecurity and poor self-esteem when it becomes excessive. Why then do individuals lack assertiveness if that is the case? Jennifer Guttman, a professional psychologist, says

People doubt themselves because they believe there are "good" and "wrong" solutions or methods. They get mired in a dilemma of second-guessing their choices and wondering whether they took the "correct" path since they think they have the ideal solution to an issue.
The world is not black and white where we live. The fact is that most of the time, there is more than one answer to a problem. It is likely that your choice was a wise one if you carefully considered your alternatives before making it. Your knowledge and instincts will usually be sufficient to complete the task on your own.

In the end, it's more important to take responsibility for your choices than those choices themselves. You don't need a crystal ball to help you make decisions since no one can foretell the future. Yes, looking back, some decisions could appear worse than others. But every decision you make with conviction will help you get closer to your true self. That is really potent all by itself.

5) Aim high, but deliver low
We all have a lot of important objectives that help us make choices and maintain our focus and motivation during our life journey. Dreams give us meaning and keep us going when things are tough. So, is having large dreams bad? Absolutely not, but there is a catch.

It's likely that you're always up against deadlines and expectations if you're an overachiever who strives too hard and sets unattainable ambitions. You may start to internalize failure when things don't go your way. That task you managed to do on schedule but which ultimately fell short of your expectations? Even if you went above and above what was required of you, it still doesn't pass the test in your mind. And if something wasn't successful, then its creator (you) must also be unsuccessful. Do you realize how damaging this kind of thinking can be to oneself?

Eventually, this perceived "failure" will have a negative impact on your self-assurance and capacity to believe in yourself and your skills. Defiance will not serve you well. You wouldn't have felt that way if your first objective had been kinder and more doable.

Sometimes, life may be really unexpected. Set smaller milestone objectives and take pleasure in the minor victories you accumulate along the route to a bigger achievement rather than establishing enormous goals and seeing failures everywhere. With each success, you gain more confidence in your capacity to reach your goals. Eventually, this self-belief will become a natural part of your everyday living. Rome wasn't constructed overnight, and that's OK!

6) Focus on your strengths Admitting that you aren't perfect at all you do is essential if you want to truly trust yourself.

Big deal that we're not all created the same way! Not everyone is a talented writer or chef. While some of us do best under moderate pressure, others thrive in competitive and demanding circumstances. Others function best when given lots of time to work alone, while others feel more productive while working in teams with their coworkers. There are 8 billion individuals on our earth, which means that there are 8 billion various ways to do tasks. This is reason to rejoice.

Even if being good at many different things may increase your confidence, it's often preferable to focus on what you do best. You set your mind at rest and leave your fears behind when you embark on projects you are certain you can achieve satisfactorily. When you start out with a good attitude, you have a considerably better chance of succeeding at anything.

This is not to say you shouldn't challenge yourself. It entails concentrating your efforts on areas where your skill set is most useful. For instance, if you're an introvert who detests public speaking, you may try asking for more speaking engagements so that you might become better at it via practice. But is the payoff from this effort truly worth the strain it would put you under? Or maybe you might concentrate your efforts on honing your skills in a field in which you are already proficient and start to really flourish.

Positive thinking has repeatedly shown that success has more to do with our state of mind than it does with achieving specific objectives. Keeping a positive attitude when dealing with life's challenges may actually lower stress and promote a better way of living.

Keep doing what you do well, have faith in your skills, and approach things your way. This does not imply that you should never try out new jobs and pastimes. Simply said, it means to focus more on the activities you believe you can become better at and less on those that are drastically outside of your comfort zone.

7) Treasure the solitude.
We don't always get as much alone time as we'd like because of how hectic and fast-paced our lives are. Constant exposure to crowded spaces and noisy situations might easily drive you mad if you're having trouble with self-trust.

There may be a feeling that you may say something stupid or act improperly at any time when there are too many people there.

Your body and mind have to put up with a lot of unneeded stress over long periods of time, and it may seem much worse in professional situations.

Spending more time on yourself will help you develop your confidence and become more at ease with your opinions. Self may have an open dialogue with the actual you by being silent and motionless. In addition to its many health advantages, meditation may teach you more about the true you that lies underneath all of your irrational concerns and expectations.

You'll gradually start to feel more at ease in your own skin as you go more into unfamiliar terrain. If you practice diligently and often, this confidence will gradually spread to other areas of your life as well.

8) Quit delaying action till later.
The quickest method to develop confidence, in the words of Margie Warrell, is to behave

just as you would if you already had it. Even if we provided many confidence-boosting suggestions and counsel, many readers still wouldn't be willing to alter their behavior.

Stop restricting yourself if you really want to be able to trust yourself. You need to push yourself outside your comfort zone right now. Not the day after tomorrow, not the next week, and not the next time you have a crucial business meeting. Now. It's impossible to expect confidence to come easily, just as it's impossible to expect your crush to unintentionally ask you out on a dreary Monday morning. You need to start developing self-trust and self-confidence before you feel ready if you really want to make a change.

You have so many wonderful ideas, but if you don't take down the wall now, the majority of them will never be implemented. That intriguing idea you've been thinking about for weeks but haven't had the courage to share with anyone? The time is now to contact your team leader and let them know what you think.

Although it's a tremendous move, you seldom have anything to lose. If everything goes as planned—which it generally does—you may take it a step further and bring the subject up at your next team meeting. Start small and gradually advance to greater ones.

Things will start to fall into place as soon as you develop the habit of gently pushing yourself. One day, when you look behind you, you'll only see molehills rather than mountains. You'll have proof of your perseverance and commitment to self-trust, and it will feel fantastic.

9) Create a frame of reference for yourself.
The internal Frame of Reference is one of the most significant indicators of self-confidence in the Fingerprint 4 Success

characteristic paradigm. A high score for this feature indicates that you have a strong sense of self-confidence and are at ease making judgments based on your own judgment and intuition.

The characteristic is associated with leadership roles and those who like managing teams and projects. You probably won't find yourself waiting for a general agreement before making judgments if you have this feature.

While personality traits take time to develop, there are practical steps you can take right away to strengthen your ability to make decisions. These include making sure your project goals are clear, defining the likely outcomes (both positive and negative) and preparing for them, and writing down your successes so you can look back on them when you're having a bad day.

Move forth and believe in yourself.
How much do you really believe in yourself? Do you struggle to express and defend your opinions when necessary? Do you often shy away from making significant choices under duress?

It's crucial to keep in mind that personalities and habits are not fixed on journeys of self-discovery like these. Self-reinvention is a constant theme in life, and even tiny adjustments to our routines or way of thinking may have significant long-term impacts. Taking on responsibility may make you feel a little uneasy right now, but every time you make a choice and deal with the results, whether they are positive or negative, you become a little stronger and more self-assured.

CHAPTER 2

Stop comparing yourself to others (Embrace yourself)

It may be quite difficult to use social media without comparing yourself to others. Your home isn't Pottery Barn-Esque enough, your clothes aren't hip enough, and your physique isn't fantastic enough. You could even start to feel inadequate as a result.

I'm also speaking to myself. I find it fascinating to see how these attractive, prosperous individuals spend their life. If I'm not cautious, I can find myself reading through the lives of these individuals I might or might not even know for hours on end each week, which makes me feel less than stellar about myself.

I set myself the objective of not comparing myself to others some years ago. It hasn't been simple, I'll tell you that much. I can examine the highlights of everyone else's life on my phone at all times, so I always know how I stack up versus other moms, wives, and speakers who also have social media accounts.

Comparisons rob us of our happiness, money, and sanity. We will continuously waste money and mental energy simply trying to stay up if we don't stop comparing ourselves to others. We must stop comparing ourselves to others since it is a losing game.

Comparison's Foundation
We are prone to compare ourselves to others for biological reasons. To determine how we compare to others, our brain employs comparison.

Comparison is one of the most fundamental ways we get a sense of who we are, what we're good at, and what we're not so good at, according to a professor of organizational behavior.

Most of the time, this computation is performed in the background in a split second without our knowledge. But it may soon become poisonous if we focus on the good points of other people's life. Because of our innate need for connection and belonging, comparing ourselves to others continuously jeopardizes our happiness, self-esteem, and mental health.

Effects of Comparing Yourself to Others in Real Life

The comparison trap has so many detrimental impacts, and I'm sure you've already experienced some of them. Here are a few examples that I've repeatedly observed:

recurring apprehensive, pessimistic, and negative thoughts (known as rumination)
an increase in anxiety and depression rates

Spending excessively in an attempt to keep up with the Joneses Research after research has proven that time spent on social media makes individuals feel worse about themselves. Our financial situation, as well as our mental health, are suffering as a result of all that negativity.

Financial misery is a result of trying to keep up with the Joneses, according to new research. And they found that neighbors were more likely to make significant, noticeable purchases and—this is insane to me—go bankrupt in communities where someone had won the lottery.

These bankruptcies, you guys, were entirely preventable. This is a heart problem rather than a financial one. Those folks suddenly felt the need for a lifestyle improvement after seeing one for their neighbors, even though they couldn't afford it.

As long as it is within your financial means, there is nothing wrong with enjoying a little luxury. You don't even truly own your stuff when you accumulate a lot of it and incur significant debt to acquire it all to impress your neighbor (in person or on Instagram); instead, it is you who is owned by it. You suddenly find yourself a slave to the things you believed would make you happy as the debt takes over and absorbs all of your money.

I don't want you to make choices based on how you see yourself about others. I want to teach you how to put on your blinders, stop comparing yourself to other people, and start living your life.

How to Stop Comparing Yourself to Others: 8 Useful Strategies

I'm still developing myself in this area. To assist me shift my focus off of other people and return it to building a life I enjoy, I can share with you some concrete actions I've made and principles I've used on my own.

1. Show thankfulness.

Everything for me was altered by this one habit. Years ago, I opened the Notes app on my phone and immediately entered three things for which I was thankful. I penned:

Early in the morning when nobody is awake. my wellbeing Coffee.

The first three things that sprang to mind were those. I didn't focus on my good fortune or spend much time contemplating it. And I did not cry. This was not a scene from a Hallmark film! I'm not even sure whether I saw any difference at the time.

And now? My only hope is that Notes app.

What began as a straightforward exercise in appreciation has expanded to include all of the joys—both significant and insignificant—that fill my life. Every morning I add to the list, and I go back to it anytime I need a reminder of God's protection and blessings in my life.

2. Harness the strength of contentment.
Being grateful makes you content, and contentment enables you to feel happy and satisfied no matter what your circumstances are. You're content with your life's circumstances and don't give a damn about what other people are doing.

That doesn't mean you don't have aspirations for the future or that you aren't trying to improve yourself from the inside out. And it most certainly doesn't imply that you're inert or that you're choosing to do nothing novel, interesting, or difficult with your life. It simply means that you stop putting all of your happiness on what you want to accomplish in the future and instead learn to be at peace with your life and appreciate what you have now.

3. Avoid comparing your life to the best moments of everyone else's.
Are you prepared for my most startling revelation to date? Real life isn't always reflected on social media. Boom. (I know you are aware of this, but have you ever given it any thought?)

Usually, it's only the highlights of someone's life, not the whole picture.

To maintain the lifestyle we believe everyone else is leading and that we are missing out on, we are expending so much financial and emotional energy. And that is harming both our financial stability and emotional wellness.

You may begin to make changes in your life and finances once you shift your attention away from them and back to your own.

4. Put your talents into focus.

You may be modest and yet be aware of your abilities, skills, and successes. Being modest doesn't need you to beat yourself up. That's a very unhealthy strategy and one of the main risks of comparison living. We feel worse about ourselves the more we contrast ourselves with others. We must stay away from that perilous trap.

Try listing your top three strengths and three things you truly like about yourself. Instead of merely writing "excellent people skills" as you might on a dry CV, elaborate. Make them your own! Here are my top three:

I act promptly. I enjoy doing things, so whether it's responding to edits on my next book or arranging dinner reservations, I'm constantly looking forward and taking action.

I cherish people. I may or might not have received the title of "friendliest" senior at Brentwood High School. Being among others has always been something I truly like! I can make others feel liked and cared for when they are around me because I have learned to embrace this strength.

I'm a fantastic infant sleep educator. Seriously. I would launch a company centered on sleep-training infants if I wasn't already doing what I do for a job. How should I put it? It's a present. It's also a nice one.

5. Rejoice for others.

We stop supporting those who are striving to succeed because we are always comparing ourselves to others. It also makes it difficult to rejoice alongside others who have done something!

So here is my test for you: Be glad for your buddy when she informs you about her new job. Join someone in their excitement as they purchase a new home. Keep the attention on the other person when they share the good news with you rather than returning it to yourself. Find both significant and modest methods to acknowledge others' achievements!

"Rejoice with those who rejoice," the Bible states (Romans 12:15, NIV). Don't let someone else's victory make you feel inferior. You may honestly appreciate their accomplishment while continuing to strive for your achievement since their success has nothing to do with you.

6. Recognize your competition rather than that of others.
Focus on your objectives rather than how you compare to others. In comparison to where you were at this time last year, where are you now? the previous five years?
I keep a diary for a variety of reasons, including the great things it does for my sanity. It helps me understand and put God's gifts in perspective. Additionally, it's a lot of fun to go back and flip through earlier notebooks to see how much I've changed.

You have developed, grown, achieved, and produced throughout the last year. Consider how much of it you've accomplished during your life. Examine your old diaries if you maintained them as I did. There is no better day than today to begin journaling if you haven't already.

7. Set time limits for yourself while using social media.

As we've been discussing, social media comparison may have a significant negative impact on our mental health. You may protect yourself by setting up the following boundaries:

Any profiles that tend to make you feel self-conscious should be unfollowed.

Set a timer for 30 minutes and indulge in some scrolling. My buddy, stop using social media when the time is up.

When you're eating supper with your family and friends, turn off your phone. Everyone will be happy when you are truly there with them!

Nobody has time for that, so don't feel pressured to respond to every remark and message.

Ask yourself why whenever you feel compelled to check social media. Do you feel uncomfortable, bored, or need approval? What can you do instead to feel better?

8. Go cold turkey on social media.

I know this from experience: If you're always comparing your life to that of others, it's almost hard to be happy with your own.

It may be necessary to put some severe blinders on for a while if you find it difficult to appreciate the benefits in your life and are often preoccupied with other people's blessings.

So, my greatest challenge to you is to turn off all social media. While you're at it, unsubscribe from all of the email newsletters that highlight everything you "miss" out on.

Spend that time and effort concentrating on your true wealth. Consider your friends, family, house, work, and all the other things that are important in your life. Find aspects of your own life that other people would find envious of. A lot of people are comparing themselves to everything you have if we are all looking at each other. Discover what those blessings are, and be thankful for what you have.

How Does Comparison Impact My Day-to-Day Life?

To determine if you have a problem with comparing yourself to others, consider the following questions:

Have you ever bought anything on Instagram on a whim?

Do your time on social media sites cause you to experience FOMO or even anxiety?

Is your default response to another person experiencing good fortune to be irritated?

Have you ever removed anything from social media after it received less feedback than you had hoped for?

Do you often check to see who has liked or seen your Facebook post or Instagram story?

There is no guilt in this if you checked yes to many of them! Just like everybody else, I'm susceptible to the comparison trap. I am equally guilty of worrying about what other people think of me.

But that's not what you and I were created for. More than just worrying, spending, and feeling like a failure, we were designed for more! I want every one of us to live our lives as we see fit.

Stop Comparing Yourself to Others Pay attention to the quality of your life rather than the number of things you enjoy.

The goal of everything you do, whether it is on social media or not, shouldn't be to keep up with the Joneses. Spending time, energy, and money seeking approval that you don't need is a result of worrying about likes. The Lord assured us in Isaiah 43:1 that "I have rescued you; I have called you by name; you are mine." I am aware that I will always suffer in comparison, just like everyone else. But those other folks who like our images are not our family. You and I both belong to a loving God.

Try journaling if you're prepared to fight back against comparison. I'm serious, I swear. This is how you put the procedures I discussed above into action daily! In only 90 days, My Contentment Journal will enable you to concentrate on your own life and develop into a happy person. I promise that keeping this notebook will make it easier for you to change your whole perspective, steer clear of comparisons, and find true satisfaction.

CHAPTER 3

Forgive Yourself and Develop Self-Compassion

We can't push ourselves to move on from difficult circumstances; it might be harmful to expect forgiveness to come easily and voluntarily. Consider using this mindfulness technique to help us make room in our hearts for forgiveness.

The expression "forgive and forget" has been used often as though getting over the hurt that other people have caused us is a simple task. To recover, we must enter a state of denial and successfully escape the pain that we have been suffering. The term is imperative, making the notion of forgiveness mandatory.

Of course, forgiving is a journey, a challenging one that often resembles a demanding spiritual discipline. We cannot instantly force ourselves to forgive;

forgiveness takes place at each person's speed and depends on the specifics of each case. What we can do is make room for ourselves to forgive, which, paradoxically enough, includes permitting ourselves to first struggle with our sentiments of resentment and suffering. When we are open and honest with ourselves about our emotions, we may urge ourselves to examine other perspectives on our suffering and realize that letting go of our grasp on rage and resentment can be a self-compassionate act.

When we accept forgiveness as a diverse, continuous, and customized process, we become more aware of the importance of our own needs in resolving conflicts.

Telling the tale, admitting what occurred, and expressing your feelings are often essential components of forgiveness. Without it, we exist in a manufactured world that is sometimes constructed from fabrication and is locked in time. I have a friend who thinks that one of the main factors in her divorce was the fact that she spoke the truth when her ex-parent husband passed away and he waxed lyrical about his ideal upbringing. She would say, "But you put your drunken parents to bed every night." "You left college early to accomplish it." His desire for a happier past took priority over their love as a result of her statements undermining the narrative he was trying to convey. It also came before his capacity to forgive his parents, the prospect of finding love, and the agony of his dashed hopes.

Reality might be the greatest obstacle to love at times. Our initial inclination may be to fight, deny, or cling to the past when our old myths and hopes are crushed. But if we let go, frequently sensitive forgiveness and the possibility of a new and different form of love fill the void.

According to Forgiveness documentary filmmaker Helen Whitney, "We speak about forgiveness as if it were one thing. Instead, we need to discuss pardons. There are as many different methods to forgive as there are individuals who need it. Therefore, there are countless—possibly infinite—circumstances in which we might exercise forgiveness. It might be more harmful than the first sensations of fury to expect it to be one action, driven by the simple need to forget and go on. When we accept forgiveness as a diverse, continuous, and customized process, we become more aware of the importance of our own needs in resolving conflicts. We shouldn't and cannot just "forgive and forget."

A Forgiveness Prayer
As both ask us to remain with our emotional states without passing judgment on them and to utilize meditation as the anchor of our attention, practicing loving-kindness and forgiving meditation are not dissimilar

from one another. Since we are not rejecting our pain or the negative deeds we've committed, these activities call for bravery.

Being present is necessary for forgiveness since it serves as a reminder that neither the person we've hurt nor who has hurt us is the same as the sentiments they are at the time.

The act of forgiving involves actively letting go of negative emotions like resentment, guilt, and wrath that may drain us if we allow them to consume us. Being present is necessary for forgiveness since it serves as a reminder that neither the person we've hurt nor who has hurt us is the same as the sentiments they are at the time.

The meditation traditionally consists of three steps:

First, you beg for forgiveness from people you have hurt; second, you offer forgiveness to those who have hurt you; and third, you practice self-forgiveness for all the times our judgmental thought patterns have caused us pain.

1) Take a comfortable seat and breathe normally. Start by doing forgiveness prayers aloud or in silence for people you have hurt. You may attempt, "If I have damaged someone, whether intentionally or unintentionally, I seek their forgiveness."

2) Take note of what appears. You could discover that asking someone for forgiveness triggers thoughts of another challenging circumstance or person. Do not ignore these emotions or ideas; instead, keep your attention on the exercise and avoid dwelling on your diversion or feeling guilty about it. Send your forgiveness in these new directions when fresh ideas come to mind.

3) After spending as much time as you wish on the first half of the contemplation, start by forgiving people who have wronged you.

Say something like, "If someone has damaged or harmed me, consciously or inadvertently, I forgive them."

4) Once again, recalling unpleasant memories might make you feel anything. You may just say, "I forgive you," when these thoughts, emotions, and memories rise to the surface.

5) In the last step, we focus on forgiving ourselves. Most of us have felt self-blame at some point, whether it was in the workplace, in a romantic relationship, or just because we were always caught up in cycles of perfectionism. I humbly ask for forgiveness for all the ways I have unintentionally or intentionally mistreated or wounded myself.

CHAPTER 4

Build Your Self-Worth and Self-Esteem (Don't worry about others' opinions)

Listening to what people have to say about you may be a significant contributor to poor self-esteem. This may be due, in part, to the fact that our sense of social acceptance affects our degree of self-esteem. When others talk poorly about us, we could feel ostracized and have lower self-esteem. So, you must stop caring about what other people think if you want to improve your self-esteem. It's simpler stated than done. Let's investigate.

How can worrying about what others think of you affect you, and what can you do to stop worrying, before we discuss the reasons why you could be doing so?

Low self-esteem may be brought on by worrying about what other people think of you. We are social creatures, and as such, we are continuously checking our social status and inclusion, according to Leary et al. (1995). Our self-image may suffer if we start thinking excessively about this.

If this is what you do, there are actions you can do to regain your self-confidence and stop worrying about what other people are thinking. I'm here to teach you how since I've been writing on self-esteem for many years, both online and in print. Go on reading!

Why is it a concern to care about what other people think?
The overwhelming bulk of the research in this area, according to Leary and Downs (1995), demonstrates that humans have a very essential need to increase and maintain our levels of self-esteem.

An excessive amount of concern about other people's opinions is a sign of poor self-esteem (Farooqi and Intezar, 2009). As a result, if you catch yourself doing this, you could be having self-esteem problems. Increasing your self-confidence and self-worth may help you worry less about what other people think of you.

Excessive anxiety about what other people are thinking about you and how they may be evaluating you can lead to negative thinking and other issues like self-consciousness. You must deal with it if you want to be more optimistic in your actions and ideas, as well as if you want to boost your self-assurance and social abilities.

The tendency to care too much about what other people think may also make you a people-pleaser, which is a concern. Numerous of us do develop a people-pleasing attitude since doing so has many good effects on both our personal and professional lives.

However, those who put too much effort into pleasing others may forget their own needs and become susceptible to manipulation.

In this faculty article, Jason Whiting provides one example of how trying to please everyone may have a detrimental impact on many parts of life and can result in despair or the dissolution of a marriage (Brigham Young University, 2016).

In other words, by allowing them to influence how you feel and act, worrying about what other people may think gives them power. To feel good about yourself again, you must restore your authority. Additionally, you must assume accountability for choices that are in your best interest. As long as your desires never cause harm to anybody else, this is not being selfish.

How to quit caring about what other people think of you
You need to appreciate your viewpoint more than what other people think if you want to improve your self-esteem and confidence. This entails putting more faith in your convictions, viewpoints, and ideas.

FOPO stands for fear of other people's opinions. FOPO can be beaten, as Michael Graves demonstrates, by implementing a program of self-awareness.

I just want to let you know that you don't need to worry about what other people may be thinking since we've all done it. I'm aware that it's feasible... So how do you alter it?

Challenge this by asking yourself why you care about what other people think. – Do you crave other people's acceptance because you lack confidence or high self-esteem?

Recognize that you are merely speculating about other people's opinions; you might be entirely wrong. You can't know what they're thinking in their hearts. Why are you being badly impacted by this guessing game?
Here's a terrific piece of advice:

1. Be respectful, but also believe in yourself
It is beneficial to be sensitive and take into account the views and emotions of others. You must, however, strike a balance between being attentive to other people's sentiments and letting go of concern for what other people think of you. After all, their opinions of you are just that—opinions. They are not the actual world.

2. Base decisions on your requirements
When you lack confidence or have poor self-esteem, you could make choices based on what other people anticipate rather than on your desires and emotions. You could hold yourself responsible for any

subsequent unhappiness. Shame may develop from self-blame... Be cautious because you could transfer this onto others and wonder why everyone is against you. This will only make matters worse. Not what you desire!

3. Give up worrying about what other people think.

Here are some ways that this could influence your thoughts and actions:

You could act in a way that others anticipate from you. You may not be being honest with yourself. You may feel as if you are depriving yourself of the freedom to live your life as you want.

Because you could worry about what other people think of you, you can find it difficult to relax in difficult social settings. As a result, you might make more errors and feel less confident. Because of this, you could find it difficult to handle criticism from others.

Public speaking may turn into a nightmare. You could pay more attention to the audience than to your performance since you can sense their interest as they watch. Instead of making you feel at ease, this could make you uneasy and tense. All because you may be interested in learning their thoughts. This results in a performance that is constrained by low self-confidence.

4. Be Firmer About Your Priorities

It's also crucial to learn how to say no and be more forceful since there are times when you should put your priorities first. How can you prioritize your own needs if you are always thinking about what other people think? Learn more today about assertiveness training, which may assist you.

5. Make your objectives

Make a list of your life's goals and decide whether or not you'll pursue each one. Don't allow other people to dictate how you ought to or ought not to behave. Own your success and accept responsibility for it.

6. Request the honest opinions of others
Ask them outright rather than presuming what they are thinking. You could get a nice surprise.

Sometimes we accept people's words at face value and may even be misunderstanding what they are truly thinking. The fact that you are acting in this manner based on false information makes what you are doing worse than handing others control over your life.

So, the goal of this phase is to get someone to elaborate on their thoughts and motivations. You will be better equipped to decide whether to consider someone else's perspective or reject it entirely if you have a better knowledge of what they believe. Don't give your authority away to others; it is yours.

Additional Suggestions to Help You Stop Worrying About What Others Might Think

When you find yourself discussing something with someone else or wondering what they think, pause, think about how you feel, and choose whether your viewpoint or theirs is more significant.

Decide that you will change. You will be halfway there once you decide to alter your mind process.

What do people think about this after downloading Start being yourself and feel good about it with a self-hypnosis program...

Just a word of warning

Do you believe that your family has abandoned you? What should you do? Experiences of this kind may significantly alter how much you worry about what others think of you. Because you didn't have enough affection in your life, you can end up being a people pleaser or worse.

Though it's possible you're not justified in thinking that others have abandoned you. In any case, you need to become stronger so that you can stop letting other people control who or what you are. It is not your fault if anything bad happens to you. If you need assistance, seek it out and make every effort to assist yourself as well. If it becomes overwhelming, seek expert advice; assistance is always accessible.

Do you recall the proverb, "Names won't harm me, but sticks and stones will shatter my bones?"

It's accurate. Why do you allow the views of others to have such a negative impact on you? Thoughts aren't harmful; you only risk being harmed if you allow them to. Keep in mind that you provide them with the authority they have over you. Only if you give them the freedom to be significant will their ideas and deeds be.

– I'm sure I wasted a lot of time worrying about what others thought of me and spent that time caged in dread and doubt. I disliked who I was. I now understand that I was incorrect the whole time. The best course of action is to boost your self-worth and confidence, and I hope that you can liberate yourself just like I did because you deserve more. Good fortune!

CHAPTER 5

Let Go of Perfectionism (learn new things by Allowing yourself to make mistakes)

If you discovered at an early age that how well you performed something—or how well you appeared—measured your worth, it's not your fault. A significant many of us did.

As you have undoubtedly seen, anxiety and perfectionism are closely related.

And it's difficult to let go of anxiousness when you've spent your whole life believing that everyone sees the worst in you.

Others may be able to take comfort in being "perfectly flawed," but that's not you.

Read on if you're prepared for some genuine assistance in overcoming perfectionism.

Perfectionists – are they insecure?

Simply said. Every perceived failure is seized onto by perfectionism, which then utilizes it to undermine your feeling of self-worth.

Chronic procrastination is a result of this perfectionism, not laziness.

Naturally, you'll want to shield yourself from feeling like a failure if you're persuaded that you can't perform anything flawlessly and that your lack of perfection makes you a failure.

Perfectionism may lead to insecurity in the following ways:

You consider what you accomplished to be a "fail" if it is not flawless.

You are a "failure" if you find fault with yourself or perform poorly.

You experience insecurity with others if they see your imperfection because you anticipate that they will judge you negatively or as being less than what you "should be."

Every time someone points out your imperfections and makes you feel undeserving of love or respect, the agony of that expectation is amplified.

You are temporarily granted a stay of execution by procrastinating. It's more difficult to escape the toxic mental conversation that perfectionism brings with it. However, it is easy to catch yourself in the act and alter your speech.

Top Nine Techniques for Letting Go of Perfection

If you or someone else struggles with perfectionism, the next nine suggestions are essential.

1. Specify your terms: What constitutes success and what constitutes failure?

Defining your terminology is one of the steps to resolving the cognitive biases that underlie perfectionism.

Failure is related to a particular action or achievement; the term was never intended to define or even characterize an individual. It refers to a deed or thing that falls short of minimum requirements.

You could see a subpar performance as a "failure to execute things precisely," but it does not imply that you are a failure.

Furthermore, rather than your whole person, perfection refers to a single achievement or object. Although you may do an action "perfectly," this does not imply that you are flawless.

If the term "failure" is used about anything you did when you're showing up and working, consider it evidence that you're acting and learning from it.

Failure does not equal weak. And you shouldn't ever have to worry about it.

2. Recognize the fear that drives your perfectionism.

Having ambitions is natural and healthy. However, if you gauge your value based on your accomplishments, your appearance, or what others think of you, you'll always feel inadequate. You will never feel as if you have improved enough.

Perfectionism stems from the idea that you are not enough and never will be.

You should also consider how others' perfectionism may have affected your upbringing and the worries that resulted from that impact.

Your parents seem to be both perfectionists. Did you regularly fail to live up to your parent's expectations?
Did you think that to be respected, you had to continually strive for perfection?

Were you pushed or encouraged to always look your best?
Every grade or accomplishment was compared to that of other kids.

3. Modify your language.
Stop labeling everyone, including yourself, as "perfect" or "imperfect."

It's beneficial to acknowledge your imperfections. However, you don't have to keep telling yourself that. Some people may even see your "I'm not perfect" as a justification for not making an effort or doing better.

Try using "I'm a work in progress" or "I'm doing the best I can" as an alternative. I'm human, you may say. I'm learning as I go, too.

Find other words to replace "perfect" while you're at it, like "great," "wonderful," or "amazing." Why even use the term "perfect" to describe anything about you or anybody else when you don't have to be?

When you use the term "perfect" to describe someone's look or an action, it simply serves to highlight your shortcomings.

4. Detect negative self-talk and fix it.
The only thing that counts isn't always what you say out loud. Perfectionists often underestimate the influence of the words they use to motivate themselves when they fall short of perfection.

These words eventually come out, often in ways that are harmful to you or other people.

Spend some time alone so that you may reflect on your thoughts about who you are, your achievements, your most recent employment, etc. You can only change harmful thinking once you are conscious of your thoughts.

Here are a few instances:

"You blew that one! Why are you acting this way?

"I see you. Anyone with morals wouldn't want to be associated with it.

"Perhaps you should give up if this is the best you can achieve."

5. Pay attention to your development and the lessons you've taken away from your errors.

Say it out loud: Making mistakes doesn't make you a failure; they're just a part of learning.

Everyone makes mistakes; what matters is whether you learn from them and how. However, every error is evidence that you're not what you "should be" if you're a perfectionist.

Despite your best efforts, you are still "not good enough."

You tell yourself, "This is another evidence that I'm a failure" or "What is wrong with me that I keep making such foolish blunders," after every error. Additionally, the tension these ideas produce makes you make more errors.

Instead, reflect on your accomplishments. You should be happy about it.

Nobody expects you to perform flawlessly the first time while you are acquiring new skills at school or work. This is why "practice" was created, which brings us to our next piece of advice.

6. Pay attention to your practice rather than "becoming flawless." Concentrate on enjoying the activity or the learning process, or what some people refer to as the "journey."

You're free to just take pleasure in learning something new without placing any pressure on yourself to be an expert. It's far more enjoyable if you approach it like a beginner who constantly has more to learn.

Gradual progress in something that makes you happy should be your objective.

Never contrast your efforts with those of a seasoned professional or anybody else. Experts have already committed blunders on their route to improving their performance. And even they sometimes make mistakes.

It's not necessary for the practice to "make perfect" (and it seldom does). Improvement comes through practice. Additionally, practicing mindfulness may help you refocus on what matters most.

7. Exercise self-compassion and forgiveness.

Start by looking at your expectations and objectives and being realistic about your capacity to achieve them. It's one thing to desire to do well on a crucial test. Another is to always strive to be the best and to hold yourself (and others) accountable when you aren't.

After that, you must forgive yourself:

Accept responsibility for not meeting unattainable expectations.
Accept responsibility for your faults.
Accept responsibility for your comparisons with others.
Accept responsibility for the negative internal discourse.
Doing this only once is insufficient. List all the things that come to mind that you haven't yet forgiven yourself for.

Self-forgiveness is the first step to healing. Forget about punishing yourself because you weren't the person you "should have been."

8. Take steps each day to increase your self-assurance.

You are aware of how it feels to accomplish something you are proud of. However, perfectionism continuously reminds you to compare your successes to those of others, undermining your pride and self-confidence.

Every day perfectionist ideas remain there, so it's critical to take steps to replace them with thoughts that boost your self-confidence.

Make a list of your accomplishments that you are proud of.
Every morning, list three positive traits about yourself.
Recite affirmations that feel good to you and give you a boost.

Daily self-care is important; keep in mind that you deserve love and kindness.
Telling yourself that you are enough as you are right now through words and deeds. Remind yourself of your strengths and accomplishments. Everything matters.

9. Live in the present and be at peace with your "now."
Instead of celebrating your flaws, focus on what makes you happy. Celebrate the newfound advantages you now possess.
Celebrate your accomplishments and everything you've learned thus far.

Love and accept the person you are right now. You should be thankful for how far you've come because it deserves it.

You may recognize the job that has to be done. But make the most of what you have and express gratitude for where you are right now.

You cannot do this if you are not living in the now, neither in the past with your errors nor in the future with an imagined self finally being allowed to rejoice.

You only have today. You simply need to be the one who shows up; everyone else is unnecessary.

CHAPTER 6

Nurture Your Relationships

Relationships aren't static; they're dynamic, living parts of our lives that need care and attention. You should take care of your relationships and invest the same time and effort you would in any other element of your life if you want to benefit from having good connections with others.

Remain in touch with your family

The hectic pace of life is one of the major obstacles for families to maintain communication. However, according to a Blue Zones study, the world's healthiest, longest-living individuals all have a trait in common: they prioritize their families. When you are unwell, family support may be a source of solace and encouragement as well as a positive factor in your health. Mimi Doe, an author who specializes in relationships and family, advises reuniting with family by forgiving minor offenses, spending time with them, and showing them love and compassion.

Of course, intimate friends are also subject to the same rules. This is crucial if you don't have surviving relatives or if you've been through trying times, like abuse, that makes it difficult for you to connect with them.

Improve your interpersonal abilities
the gratifying lady standing with her hands over her heart with a smile on a white backdrop
demonstrate gratitude
One of the easiest to reach pleasant emotions is gratitude, and its benefits may improve close friendships and romantic partnerships. According to 2010 research, showing thankfulness to a spouse may improve the bond between the two of you. Both the giver and the receiver of gratitude benefit from this relationship improvement. Remembering to express gratitude when a

friend lends you their ear or when your partner gives you a cup of coffee may start a chain reaction of intimacy, trust, and love.

Become forgiving

Relationships sometimes have conflicts or betrayals, but how you choose to respond to the pain may have a significant impact on how quickly the wounds heal. There are several advantages to choosing forgiveness, both material and spiritual. According to Fred Luskin, director of the Stanford Forgiveness Project, it's simpler to let go of the resentment or hurt feelings brought on by a situation if you keep in mind that most of your suffering is caused by the emotions and thoughts you are experiencing as you think back on the incident, rather than the event itself.

Be sympathetic

Being compassionate means being open to yourself and others—even during difficult times—while maintaining a kind, nonjudgmental attitude. Whether it's a love relationship, friend, family member, or work colleague, when you feel compassion for someone, you allow for greater communication and a closer connection. This does not include bearing others' pain or feeling their feelings. Instead, compassion is the act of seeing when another person is dissatisfied or that their needs aren't being fulfilled and being moved to act in their favor. Being imitative animals, we respond with compassion when it is exhibited to us.

Embrace others

Accepting the other person in the relationship is also crucial. This does not apply in abusive or unhealthy control circumstances when your priority should always be your protection. Instead of passing judgment on someone, try to understand where they are coming from. Accept the other's strengths and flaws realistically, just as you would for yourself, and keep in mind that change happens through time.

Make rituals together

It's simple to wander away from pals due to hectic schedules and the availability of online social media that provides the appearance of actual touch. You have to put out an effort to connect to foster the intimacy and support of friendships. Tom Rath, a Gallup researcher, discovered that individuals who make time for events or vacations intentionally have more good vibes and better connections. Making a routine that you can participate in and that doesn't add to your stress is a simple method to do this. For example, sharing a stroll during lunch breaks or chatting on the phone on Fridays are two ways to stay in touch with the people who matter to you the most.

The happiest people are those that spend 6-7 hours each day socializing (which might include hanging out with friends, eating meals with family, or even emailing a coworker). People who don't socialize at all (or who engage in an exhaustive amount of social time) feel more anxious. Maintaining balanced, healthy relationships as well as emotional wellness might depend on knowing when to give time to others and when to take time for yourself.

Try a guided meditation on forgiveness.
There are three stages in this guided practice of forgiving: We start with people who have been harmed by us, whether on purpose or accidentally. We then focus on individuals who have similarly harmed us, whether on purpose or accidentally. Finally, we focus on forgiving ourselves for any purposeful or inadvertent ways we may have damaged ourselves. This procedure may be repeated as frequently as you want with the same or other individuals.

CHAPTER 7

Practice Self-Care (Put yourself first)

5 Tips For Best Self-Care

Even though you are aware of how important it is to take care of yourself, do you know exactly how to prioritize your needs in your life? Nutrition is not the only factor in nourishment (although obviously, good nutrition is one of the most fundamental building blocks of looking after yourself). It also includes taking care of your bodily, emotional, and spiritual needs. We are so excited to share with you our top 5 tips for prioritizing your health, happiness, and contentment.

Top 5 Strategies for Prioritizing Your Own Life

FIRST Learn to Create Healthy Boundaries
There are people who would attempt to persuade you that attending to your own needs before those of others is selfish, which

might sometimes seem like it is. But it is clearly not the case!

It makes sense to take good care of "you". You must first take care of yourself in order to be able to assist people you love as best you can before you can take care of others.

Getting in the habit of saying "no thanks" rather than "yes" is one of the simplest ways to start establishing healthy boundaries (especially when yes would be out of a sense of duty).

Over-giving out of a feeling of duty or accountability often results in disappointment and exhaustion. Giving to others out of a well-informed and sincere desire to become engaged develops both you and the people you're giving to. This implies that you prioritize yourself while still showing up in healthy ways for others. Win-win situation!

Two: Begin each day with something special for you.

Get to the gym or start your run as soon as you wake up if maintaining your fitness is your first priority. Start your day by focusing on developing calm, and then gradually include meditation in your routine. Make room for a calm cup of coffee if that's what you need to start your day.

It doesn't have to be detrimental to anything else; for instance, if you want to become a writer, set your alarm for 30 minutes earlier and use that time to write.

fresh day

Give it your all.

Obey your first priority.

On the other hand, keep in mind that until YOU make it a priority, it won't ever be one. This won't be done for you by anybody.

If you begin each day by focusing on your top priority, you will set the tone for the rest of the day and the rest of your life.

Decide on your priorities and incorporate them into your daily schedule. Then see how everything else flows naturally into place. Your life will begin to empty of distractions and unnecessary items, leaving just the things that have far more significance and purpose for you.

3. Finish the task you've been putting off!
You are familiar with the nagging sensation that comes from putting off something that you know you should be doing for yourself but are putting off.

Perhaps you spend your free time on other tasks, such as household duties, work for other people, and other activities that appear to be necessary. But will they really have mattered in 10 years? Most likely not!

You need to do that thing for yourself that you are resisting because it will matter in 10 years. You are at odds with what really matters to you if you procrastinate or delay essential personal objectives.

It helps to open up the rest of your life when you finally accomplish whatever it is you are putting off, like enrolling in that yoga or dancing class. It creates a feeling of possibility, productivity, inspiration, and drive that will permeate all of the other spheres and interactions in your life.

You start to feel upbeat and motivated, and you're able to be a lot more resourceful and healthier when you're able to be there for others as well as yourself.

Four: Become quite clear about what you want.

Having a firm understanding of your goals can motivate you. Here is a quick method to help you identify your motivation.

Start with this query and some paper and a pen:

What exactly about __________ is significant to me?

Take this drill at least seven questions deep. Keep it straightforward and go with the first reaction that comes to mind for each.

For instance, if working remotely is one of your goals, start by asking:

What specifically about "working from home" matters to me?

Perhaps the best response is, "So I can manage my time." After that, you pose the following query:

What specifically does "controlling my time" matter to me?

Fundamentally, it is up to you to identify your values, and from there, your drive will naturally flow. Your drive to strive for your goals stems from a genuine connection to the inner desires you have for yourself.

Five: Show yourself some love.
Although it may seem apparent, self-care begins with you, even in the slightest details like the way you speak to yourself. If things don't go your way, it's simple to be harsh on yourself.

Be nice to yourself the next time you spill coffee or drop a phone by paying attention to how you say to yourself. As you would a close friend, speak to yourself. You may take care of yourself by talking positively to yourself. Consider a younger version of yourself as the person you are speaking to and treat yourself with the same care and compassion you would a kid.

Take some time to treat yourself kindly and on a practical level. For example, take a bath with your favorite oils, bath salts, or pampering items. Treat yourself to a movie or go out and have a great hot chocolate.

Be considerate. Be kind. You need to nurture yourself most by putting yourself first!

CHAPTER 8

Do What You Love and Love What You Do

You may be aware of the value of taking care of yourself, but do you know exactly how to make yourself the center of your own life? Food and nutrition are not the only sources of nourishment (although obviously, good nutrition is one of the most fundamental building blocks of looking after yourself). Maintaining your physical, emotional, and spiritual well-being is another aspect of nourishment. To put yourself first and live the healthiest, happiest, and most pleasing life possible, we are eager to share with you our top 5 strategies.

One: Recognize and Establish Healthy Boundaries
There are some who may attempt to persuade you that attending to your own

needs before those of others is selfish. It's clearly not the case, however!

The common sense part is taking care of "you." To care for others, one must first care for oneself. This will leave one with the energy and resources necessary to provide the greatest assistance possible for the people they love.

By practicing saying "no thanks" rather than "yes," one of the simplest ways to begin establishing healthy boundaries is (especially when yes would be out of a sense of duty).

Out of a feeling of duty or responsibility, those who overgive often experience disappointment and exhaustion. Giving from a genuine desire to be engaged and from a place of strength supports both you and the people you are giving to. In other words, you prioritize yourself while still presenting yourself in healthy ways for others. It benefits both parties in a positive way!

Two: Begin each day with a gift for yourself. The moment you wake up, get to the gym or go for a run if maintaining your fitness is your top priority. You should ease into your meditation practice if you find that establishing quiet helps you start your day. Make room for it to happen if you need a calm cup of coffee to start your day.

If you want to become a writer, for instance, set your alarm for a half-hour earlier and dedicate that time to writing. It doesn't have to be to the exclusion of everything else.

new day

Make it yours.

Own the priority.

Alternatively, keep in mind that if YOU don't make it a priority, it won't ever be a priority. Nobody will carry out this task on your behalf.

You are setting the tone for the rest of your day and the rest of your life if you begin each day with your top priority.

Make a list of your priorities and incorporate them into your everyday activities. Then see how the rest flows naturally into the first. Your life will gradually fill up with all those things that have a lot greater value and importance for you as the distractions and stuff you don't need leave it.

Do The Task You've Been Postponing!
You've had that nagging sensation when you have something you should be doing for yourself but are delaying it because it seems important.

You could be spending your free time on tasks that appear to be necessary, such as household duties, work for others, and other things. Will they really have mattered 10 years from now? doubtless not!

What you need to do for yourself is the thing you are rejecting and the thing that will matter in 10 years. You are in conflict with what really matters to you if you are putting off or postponing crucial personal objectives.

The rest of your life will become more accessible after you finally accomplish whatever it is you are putting off, like enrolling in that yoga or dancing class. It creates a feeling of possibility, productivity, inspiration, and drive that will spread to your other spheres of influence and connections in life.

As a result of being able to show up for yourself and others in a far more resourceful and wholesome manner, you start to feel upbeat and motivated.

Get Very Specific About Your Goals in Number Four
Having motivation is a result of being motivated by your goals. An easy method to help you identify your motivation is provided here.

Start with the following inquiry and some paper and a pen:

"What do you think is significant to me?"

Explore this activity for at least seven questions. Keep it simple and rely on the first thought that each answer generates.

If, for instance, working remotely is your objective, start by asking the following questions:

Why is it vital to me to "work from home"?

To better manage my time, maybe the reply. In light of it, you pose the following query:

Why is it vital to me to "manage my time"?

In essence, you get to discover your values, and then your drive flows directly from them. Your will to strive for your goals stems from a genuine connection to the self-serving motivations behind them.

5. Take care of yourself.
Although it may seem apparent, self-care begins with you and can be shown in even the simplest of ways, like the way you speak to yourself. If something doesn't go your way, it is easy to be harsh on yourself.

Take note of how you speak to yourself the next time you spill coffee or drop your phone, and be gentle to yourself. Like you would a trustworthy friend, speak to yourself. When it comes to taking care of yourself, positive self-talk will assist you a lot. Consider a younger version of yourself as the person you are speaking to, treating yourself with the same consideration and love you would treat a kid.

Put simply, give yourself some loving attention by taking the time to pamper yourself. Use your favorite bath salts, oils, or other spa-quality items. Enjoy a movie or treat yourself to a great hot chocolate.

Be compassionate. Be considerate. The most important nutrition for you is prioritizing your needs.

Conclusion

Even if you don't feel especially strong, consider your progress and resilience. You are alive and very strong right now, where you are. Also, practice self-compassion. Self-love may not come easily. But it will eventually get ingrained in your heart.

Yes, you could suffer, but when you look back on these times, you'll realize that they served as stepping stones on your path to becoming the finest version of yourself.

www.ingramcontent.com/pod-product-compliance
Lightning Source LLC
Chambersburg PA
CBHW070546160726
48003CB00005B/1921